Finding Light In The Wild

Poems for the soul

Chrissy Pettengill

/ BookLeaf
Publishing

India | USA | UK

Made with ❤ on the BookLeaf Publishing Platform
www.bookleafpub.in
www.bookleafpub.com

Dedication

To every person who wishes for peace on Earth.

Preface

Finding Light in the Wild is a collection born in
moments of stillness. Moments found beneath the shade
of a tree, or sat beside a gently flowing creek. Moments
of grief, and of pure love. These poems are pieces of me,
etched from the soul and onto these pages. Memories
that have shaped me into the person I am today, and my
view of the beauty and the pain of this life. My longing
for peace amongst us all, always searching for the light.

This book is for anyone who has ever sought peace in
the forest, solace in the sunrise, and love in unexpected
places.
May you find within these pages, a reflection of your
own unconditional love for Earth and for us all. Knowing
that even in the darkest moments, light is waiting to
peak through.

With love and gratitude,
Chrissy Pettengill

Acknowledgements

To my family and friends —your encouragement is
everything to me. Your unconditional love has shaped
me into the person I am today, and I am so grateful.

To all of those who continue to strive for peace— I love
you. Thank you.

To nature— for your never ending beauty and
inspiration, for healing me, and grounding me.

To every reader holding this book— may these words
inspire you, and ignite your light within.

With endless gratitude,
Chrissy Pettengill

1. The Stranger

Driving country roads on a beautiful day,
i pass by a stranger walking.
In my head, I wish for them the absolute best.
I wish for their safety.
I hope that their belly is full.
I pray that they have somewhere to go.
I plead with a higher power that they feel loved.

Oh stranger, it does not matter who you are.
For you, I want
what I want
for us
all.

2. Becoming a Mom

What started with chaos,
ended with immeasurable joy.

There he was, safe in my arms.
His eyes so blue, locked with mine.

The world shifted then and there,
for a new little soul had arrived.

Bringing with him,
all the light.

The light that went out,
just shy of 3 months prior.

When our family lost a dear soul,
and with that,
it all went dark.

I can't pretend to understand how it all works,

but I know that we were all
meant to survive this.

I lost my brother before becoming a mom,
but it made me who I am today.

Although gone from this physical plane,
we are all connected by love.

Family forever.
In this life,
and the next,
and the next.

3. Different, not less.

It is always interesting to me
how people have opinions
about situations they have never experienced.

About people they have never met,
places they have never been,
lives they have not lived.

Some people want to paint Autism as a tragedy.
They want you to think our lives are miserable,
that this is really something to be afraid of.

I wonder if they would say that if they saw the way
my son's eyes light up when the wind hits his face.
How he flaps his hands and laughs with glee for
experiencing the true beauty that is nature.

Or maybe they would feel differently if they saw
saw him jumping for joy after he organizes his markers
into

the perfect line, and then breaks out into a dance party,
even if there is no music.

I think it would really hit them when they saw him
squint his eyes
and rub his chin into the person he is next to,
in the special little way that he shows love.

Autistic or not, we all have struggles.
What would help the most, is support and inclusivity
for those who are different.

We all have things to learn from different life
experiences,
and what my son has taught me most is pure
unconditional love.
After all, love is always the answer.

4. Finding peace

Barefoot in a shallow stream.
The water flows gently past smooth rocks,
covered in deep green moss,
and adorned with tiny fungi.

The sunlight peaks through the canopy of
leaves above you, revealing marvelous rays
of light that shine down from the heavens.

You take in a deep breath as you listen to
the sounds of the water, and the gentle
rustling of wind through the leaves.

You are at peace in the forest,
and the trees welcome you.

Nature's energy touches your soul,
and reminds you what is sacred.

5. The Abandoned House

I stand tall amongst the trees,
though my bones may sag a bit.

When the wind whistles through my broken windows,
I creak and moan against the night sky.

Ivy clings and wraps around my body,
helping to hold me up after all these years.

My front door slowly opens to reveal a grand staircase
enveloped
in cobwebs, and a layer of dust and grime.

I call out to you with each creaking groan
of my tired bones.

I wish to tell you the memories I hold inside these walls.
Each story etched into my essence.

6. Memories

When I think of you,
I think of your smile.

I think about the countless laughs we shared,
and the arguments, too.

I think of your incredibly kind spirit,
and how you were a friend to everyone.

I think of how you always had my back,
no matter what.

I think we both know that I
do enough thinking...

But I'll think of you always,
until we meet again.

7. That Fall Feeling

It feels like that time again,
as a golden sunset illuminates trees of red.

The air feels crisp, and the breeze brings
leaves cascading down.

An inviting path weaving through maples and
evergreens leads to
a bonfire glowing in the dusk.

The smell of cider and pumpkin wafts into the air, as
friends
laugh and hold each other close, reminiscing through the
night.

8. The Moon

An owl's wings bathed in my light

Shadows dancing on the forest floor

The sun has gone, it's time for night

Waters coming into shore

Like diamonds I shine upon each wave

The ocean is full of stars

Bringing the solitude you crave

Counting all your scars

Like memories that come back each night

Tucking you into bed

Glowing, shining, oh so bright

Rest your weary head

9. The Edge

Standing on the edge

A vast landscape below

Rocks turn into trees

Turn into rivers

Turn into roads

Does anybody see what I see

Or do they only see what they know

Losing my grip

One slip at a time

Sending rocks flying

The more I keep trying

If I give up

Will anybody know

10. Lead with love

Gentle I remain

Though the world is harsh around me

Trying to stay sane

Can't admit I'm drowning

Tears fall down my face

And I beg the skies above

To help the human race

To let us lead with love

I know that we can do it

We can evolve and be at peace

Let us all take hands

All fire must cease

11. That One Place

You know that one place

Between dreaming and waking

Your soul dancing out of your body

Somehow it feels even more real than this

Like maybe it's where we find clarity

A conversation with a loved one lost

An epiphany on what choice to make

A feeling of connection we have since forgotten

A risk we are too scared to take

The sensation of a rising frequency

The vibration of everlasting love

Knowing we are all connected

Held by the clouds above

12. Being different

I remember when I learned that I was different

And people wanted to make sure I knew

They said it like it was a bad thing

But deep down, I felt that wasn't true

For the contrast in us all makes the world beautiful

Like snowflakes, each of us unique

Different faces, different backgrounds, different stories to
tell

Without this, the world would be bleak

So I celebrate who I am, and who you are, too.

Let us love ourselves fully, let us be true.

13. Earth Is A Woman

Earth is a Woman

And Earth is a mother

She gives us her all

In hopes we will love her

But through greed and destruction

We rape and degrade her

Simultaneously praising the one we think made her

She is fighting back with wind and rain

fire and lava

expressing her pain

She continues to give

While we continue to take

How much longer

Until she breaks

Love Mother Earth as she loves you

and she will bring blessings anew

Let her flourish and grow in hues of green

revealing levels of beauty unseen

14. Holding on

Losing somebody while they are still alive

Is a pain that cuts so deep

Addiction has them in its grips

All you can do is weep

How do you get through to the person you know

When they feel like they are no longer there

You cry, you beg, you show tough love

Screaming that it isn't fair

Even if they can't hear you now

Please don't give up the fight

Nobody is too far gone to be helped

Just be there, and be their light

For their soul still shines inside them

Asking to be set free

From the pain the drugs have caused them

Its not who they want to be

15. Speak up

Remember to continue to use your voice

in a world where we still have the choice

Will you stand for those who cannot stand

Speak for those who cannot speak

Will you help those who cannot be helped

Will you always practice what you preach

Can you be a friend in times of need

A listening ear

Or a heart without greed

Do you wish for all,

food to eat

a roof over their heads,

and a bed to sleep

For a world without kindness

to everyone around

Is a world slowly burning

to the ground

16. Art saves

I was thinking today about how art can save

The eyes it can open

And the roads it may pave

The way it can make loneliness disappear

Or remind you of somebody near and dear

The way we are moved by a poem, or a song

By a painting, or a dance

And can feel we belong

Bringing creative energy

To those all around

Filling the Earth

With beautiful sound

Let us never forget

The importance of art

As it brightens our lives

And brings peace to the heart

17. My Baby Boy

When I'm old and grey

And thinking back on life

I'll reminisce about these times

When you were small enough for me to hold

And you would keep me up through the night

What seems tough now

Will be the sweetest memory

So I'll never, ever take it for granted

I'll just hold your tiny body in mine

And wish that I could stop time

And though you will grow

Likely bigger than I

You will always be my baby boy

18. Realities of War

A child cries out

Walking barefoot amongst rubble

Of what was once a neighborhood

Their skin is covered in dirt and ash

Their family still lies in the debris

Every day the child wanders

Hoping somebody will come to save them

There is no food

There is no water

Their hope dwindles

The war has taken everything

And with each shaking breath

The child asks the sky

Can you see us?

Please see us...

19. Kindness and connection

I like the people who stumble on their words when they
are filled with passion

The ones who safely capture a bug and put it back
outside

They wear their heart on their sleeve for all to see

And we need more of this in mankind

Like when you see two strangers helping one another

And you almost feel filled with pride

That the connection between humans hasn't fully been
lost

After everything it still hasn't died

Leading with compassion and love will bring us to great
heights

Evoking peace within us all

Remember to always be kind to your neighbor

For united we stand

And divided we fall

20. Taking off the mask

Learning who you really are

After taking off the mask

Peeling off the layers

Preparing for the task

Like being given permission

To be who you always were

Now that there is a label

Nobody will deter

Release the energy inside

Fight for justice

And do not hide

The difference in your thinking

Is needed more than ever

In a world that can doubt you

Show them that you're clever

Do not doubt yourself

For who you are is a gift

Barriers will be broken down

And minds you will shift

21. Death is not goodbye

Death is an illusion

Of goodbyes and last times

Questions we can't answer

Senses we can't define

And though their flesh has gone

We feel their presence still

In the wind that whistles through the trees

While basking on the hill

When a question presses in our head

And we wonder what they might say

We hear their answer in our mind

Assuring us it's ok

And it feels like they are sharing a smile

When you see a rainbow in the sky

Like they put it there just for you

Urging you not to cry

www.ingramcontent.com/pod-product-compliance
Lightning Source LLC
Chambersburg PA
CBHW050950030426
42339CB00007B/371